AMAZING RACING

FORMULA ONE CARS

BY ASHLEY GISH

CREATIVE EDUCATION · CREATIVE PAPERBACKS

Published by Creative Education and Creative Paperbacks
P.O. Box 227, Mankato, Minnesota 56002
Creative Education and Creative Paperbacks are imprints of
The Creative Company
www.thecreativecompany.us

Design by The Design Lab
Production by Joe Kahnke
Art direction by Rita Marshall
Printed in China

Photographs by Alamy (Dave Hewison Sports, dpa picture alli-
ance archive, GP Library Limited, speedpix), Getty Images (Jon
Feingersh/Stone, Keystone-France/Gamma-Keystone), iStockphoto
(chromatika), Newscom (JOHN SIBLEY/REUTERS), Shutterstock
(Ev. Safronov, Abdul Razak Latif, Steven Marques, SpazGenev,
Vdant85), SuperStock (mirafoto/imageBROKER)

Library of Congress Cataloging-in-Publication Data
Names: Gish, Ashley, author.
Title: Formula One cars / Ashley Gish.
Series: Amazing racing cars.
Includes webography. Includes index.
Summary: A fast-paced, high-interest introduction to Formula One
cars, aerodynamic race cars known for their wings and use in
closed circuit races. Also included is a biographical story about
Formula One driver Lewis Hamilton.
Identifiers: LCCN: 2019049503
ISBN 978-1-64026-287-4 (hardcover)
ISBN 978-1-62832-819-6 (pbk)
ISBN 978-1-64000-417-7 (eBook)
Subjects: LCSH: Formula One automobiles—Juvenile literature. /
Automobiles, Racing—Juvenile literature. / Automobiles—Juvenile
literature.
Classification: LCC TL236.265.G57 2021 / DDC 629.228/5—
dc23

CCSS: RI.1.1, 2, 4, 5, 6, 7; RI.2.2, 5, 6, 7, 10; RI.3.1, 5, 7, 8;
RF.1.1, 3, 4; RF.2.3, 4

First Edition HC 9 8 7 6 5 4 3 2 1
First Edition PBK 9 8 7 6 5 4 3 2 1

Table of Contents

Formula One cars are race cars. Teams build their own cars. They must follow special rules, or a "formula." Formula One cars are also called Formula 1 or F1 cars.

Formula One cars are much lighter than normal cars.

Formula One can be dangerous. More than 50 drivers have died while racing or practicing since 1952. The sport is safer now than it was in the past. Drivers wear helmets and protective suits.

F1 cars have many safety features to protect drivers in scary situations.

*The car's front wing
pushes down on air to
keep the car on the road.*

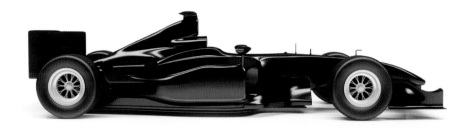

Formula One cars are

aerodynamic. Moveable wings create

downforce. Downforce moves air quickly

under the wings and slowly over them.

This pushes the car down toward the road.

It improves tire **traction**.

aerodynamic having a shape that allows air to move smoothly over
the surface

traction the grip of a tire on the ground

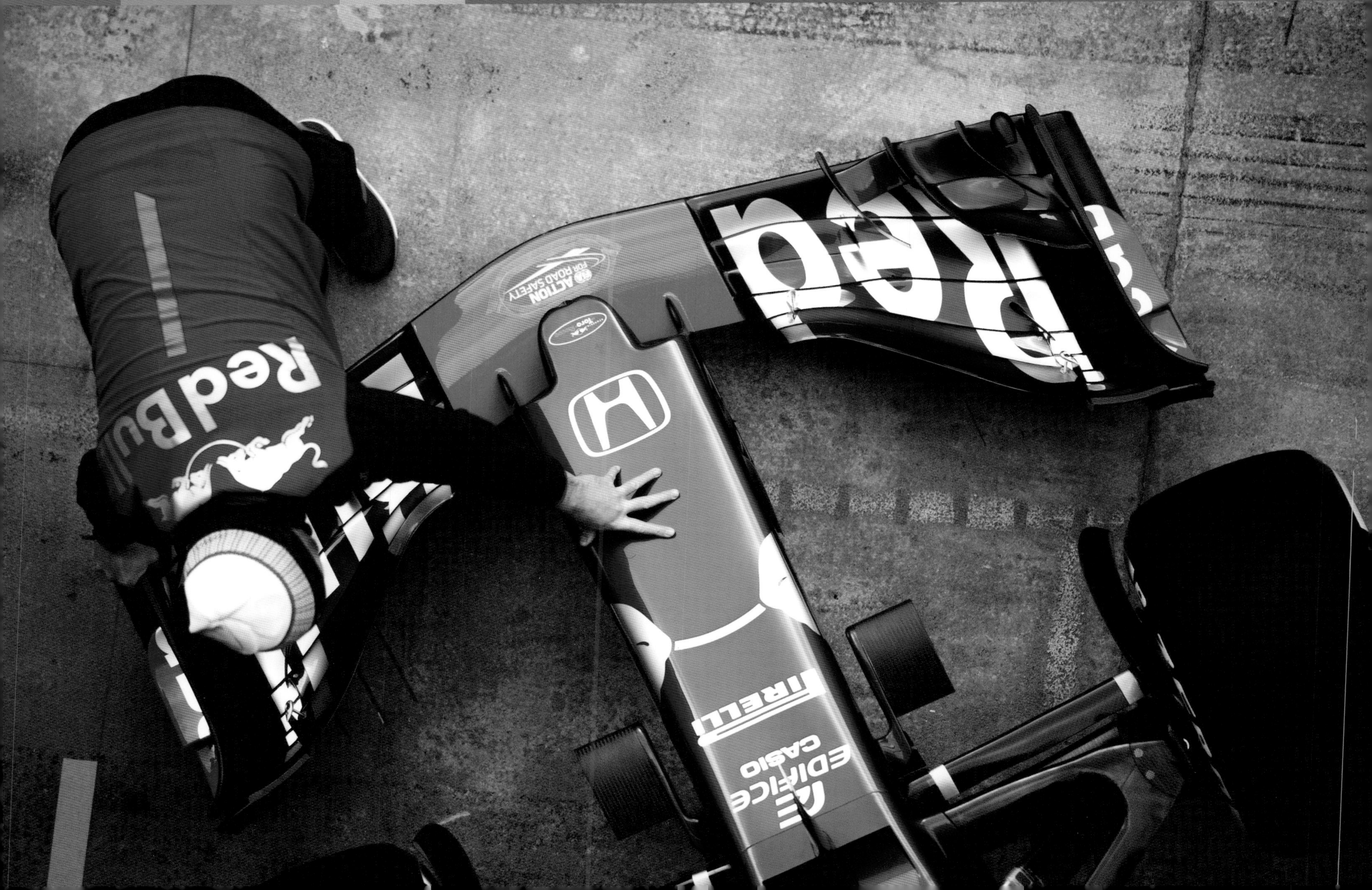
ACTION
FOR ROAD SAFETY
EDIFICE
CASIO

*The tires of most racing cars
are filled with nitrogen gas.*

Parts inside an F1's lightweight engine move three times faster than a regular car's. Formula One engines wear out quickly. They usually last just one season.

engine   a machine that makes a vehicle move by burning fuel

Drivers in the 2019 British Grand Prix raced 52 laps and 190 miles (306 km).

A Formula One race is called a **Grand Prix** (*pree*). Drivers practice on Friday and Saturday. On Saturday afternoon, drivers race in **qualifying sessions**. The race is held on Sunday.

Grand Prix a French phrase that means "great prize"

qualifying sessions races that determine the starting order of the official race

Many companies pay to put their names or logos on F1 cars.

Grands Prix take place on road circuits. Some circuits are public roads that have been closed off for the race. F1 races must be longer than 189.5 miles (305 km). Drivers race around the circuit for up to two hours.

circuits closed routes that begin and end in the same place

Melbourne
Australia

The Formula One World

Championship season begins in Melbourne,
Australia. It tours all over the world.
Points are awarded at the end of each race.
The team with the most points wins the
world championship.

*In 2019, the F1 season
included 21 Grands
Prix around the globe.*

In 1950, Giuseppe Farina won the first Formula One World Championship. The Italian racer won by just three points!

Farina (above) beat out 20 other drivers from 9 different countries in 1950.

*Each F1 car has a pit
crew of about 20 people.*

If you watch a Formula One race, you might see a car's tires get so hot that they fall apart on the track. The **pit crew** changes the tires in about three seconds. Then the car zooms back to the track!

pit crew the team of people that fixes cars during a race

Driver Spotlight: Lewis Hamilton

Lewis Hamilton was born in Stevenage, England, in 1985. At the age of eight, he started racing karts. By the time he was 22, Lewis was racing Formula One cars. Many racing experts and fans say he is the best driver in Formula One history. Through 2019, Lewis had won six world championships and earned more career points than any other F1 driver.

Read More

Bodensteiner, Peter. *Formula 1 Cars*. North Mankato, Minn.: Black Rabbit Books, 2017.

Silverman, Buffy. *How Do Formula One Race Cars Work?* Minneapolis: Lerner, 2016.

Skinner, Adam. *Fast Forward: The World's Most Famous Race Tracks and Race Cars*. Minneapolis: Wide Eyed Editions, 2019.

Websites

Easy Science for Kids: F1 Car Facts
https://easyscienceforkids.com/best-f1-car-aerodynamics-video-for-kids/
Learn what makes Formula One cars go fast.

Kiddle: Michael Schumacher Facts for Kids
https://kids.kiddle.co/Michael_Schumacher
Read about one of the most famous Formula One racers.

KidzSearch: Formula One
https://wiki.kidzsearch.com/wiki/Formula_One
Learn more about Formula One racing.

Note: Every effort has been made to ensure that the websites listed above are suitable for children, that they have educational value, and that they contain no inappropriate material. However, because of the nature of the Internet, it is impossible to guarantee that these sites will remain active indefinitely or that their contents will not be altered.

Index